downed lines

First Edition

ISBN: 979-8-218-04276-9

Cover photo: Madison County, Iowa – Winter 1961

Cover art courtesy of Cal Sharpe, Caligraphics

To:

Mary Jane
and
Bailey

Table of Contents

My sleepless night

At 2:47 AM,
the bed shakes
and I wake.
My body is cold.
The sheets are tired.

I tell her there has
been an earthquake
and the Cumbre Vieja
volcano has just dropped
179 million tons
of rock into the Atlantic.

She says:
"It's not an earthquake —
there are no earthquakes in
Florida – at least not in
the middle of winter – it's
not earthquake season."
But I look out the
upstairs window,
east, toward
the ocean.

The wall of water, I say
could be up to 110 feet
tall – maybe taller.

Go back to sleep she says.
There's no earthquake,
and there are no water walls.
And don't mention the

Cumbre Vieja again —
tonight.

But I can't sleep so I go to the
kitchen to make tea.

I sit on a stool by the
bar watching TV while a
weather girl in a
lavender dress
explains that
the day ahead
will be just like
the last – 82 degrees,
partly
cloudy,
no rain,
no
earthquakes,
tsunami risk is low.

I watch until
I weary of her cheer,

and then
I switch to a 24 Hr. news channel
where a grave, but
engaging, field reporter is
broadcasting live from
a war-torn foreign country
and I am
cold again.

Star gazing on Miami Beach

I looked at the stars
last night and I saw Saiph
winking at me – like she does –
– the little nymph…only 730 light
years southeast of Miami Beach.
Oh you shouldn't have – you
waif…you should have waited
until I could join you out there
in the Universe…we could have
waltzed among the stars,
we could have gone to the
ends of the earth together,
or maybe to the end of the heavens,
poking fun at the light years,
jesting of time and space,
putting them both in their place.
We could have prodded
old Orion to pick up the pace.
We could have instructed Neptune
to take it out back and get it out
of his system and we could
have asked the Universe
if the great God is listening.
Time is fleeting… it's between you
and me now.
No need to inform the others.
Lie back upon your Jimmy Buffett
inspired beach blanket, my Love.
Wait for the full moon to rise over
the ocean.

Reflections on traffic

Traffic sucks – it's woven into
the fabric of American life
like caraway seed bagels
and yacht rock - Chanel perfume &
the Doobie Brothers. All taken
for granted and running in the
background. The
streets will soon be taken over
by self-piloting tractor trailers.
And urban hipsters on
robotic hoverboards
will vie for cramped automated
space in tiny, inflated houses.

Put me in my container
now. Sail me out past the
Continental Shelf and sink me
alongside the surplus WW II
jeeps, & 45 automatic pistols, no bone
to pick or soul to sell.

The last exit ramp is blocked by a
wildfire, and there is no way
we make it
home tonight.

Writer's rules

Do you write every day?
she asked me.
They say you must
write every day to be
any good.

Sometimes I write every
day, sometimes I don't,
I told her.

One time I wrote for
a week straight. But I
was drunk then and
none of it made sense.

Then I wrote for a month straight:

I wrote all about my day
I wrote about my night
I wrote down what time I got up
I wrote about what I ate
I wrote about what I drank
I wrote about the weather
I wrote a letter to myself
I wrote a list

of my ten favorite poems

I wrote down what time I went to bed…
…and what I dreamed about…

Did you dream about me? she asked.

At the beach in November

I'm at the beach in November,
six weeks before the Season begins.
I watch waves break.
I count the cadence.
I count the period: five seconds, six seconds apart.
They aren't restricted by
any laws of man, these waves.
They answer to only the wind
and the moon.

To be killed by a wave is to be killed
directly by God, or so I am told. –
It's called an act of God.
Why God would be involved
in such an act I'll never know.

I time the waves with my Aquastar.
The east wind is in my face,
and I adjust my dark glasses
to better inspect a container ship on the horizon.
It is travelling south toward the Panama Canal.
And then maybe on
to Singapore,
or to Malaysia
or to Japan.
Another load of sand
or soybeans –
lumber –
farm machinery –
household goods –
bed sheets.

I am sure the ship
is manned by sturdy sailors –
Germans or Lebanese, or Norwegians,
all sailing on God's waves,
thinking of wives or girlfriends
or small children left behind in
far away ports.
Unlike me, they are unafraid and sailing.

At the VA: 1968

Live each day like it's your last,
and someday you will be right.
Says Granddad – a man in his
77th year…as I was entering my 12th.
After that:
A Doctor enters the day room
of the VA hospital,

Doc crushes his
cigarette in the ashtray near the
door. It's a clove cigarette doc says.
Piss poor excuse for a smoke.
Chesterfields are a smoke.

Then:
Who's the young man asks doc.

My grandson – says Granddad.
Granddad looks pale.
I say:
I hope we can go home soon and
hunt rattlesnakes in the timber behind the house.
Someday grandpa says.

I want to plant corn in the spring he tells me.
So do I, I tell him.

Knee high by the fourth of July.
he tells me.

Corn planting knowledge will serve me
well in years to come.

A hotel clerk in Colorado insulted your
grandmother on our honeymoon in
1920 he tells me.

Poor guy didn't know grandpa.
The story trails off…

*

Doc leaves and
darkness gathers.
We talk about
the War (again)
the Big One.

We talk about the Navy.
When you get old enough,
join the Navy, he advises.
Never join
the Army.
Too much marching
in the Army.
A guy is free on the ocean.

I promise him I will never join
the Army.

Ever.

A tale of two souls

I looked through
the glass once, and I noticed
your soul moving quietly
wonderfully, methodically
from room to room
occasionally pausing to
move some small piece
of furniture, to try on
new clothes, to adjust
'Cupid with Butterfly'
above the headboard,
to return Kant to the
bookshelf, and
to position the blinds for
late afternoon sun…

…and you have
caught me too, an Old Soul
with creaky bones and
hardened liver, moving
cautiously down the steps
to the basement, groping
in the dark, hoping to find
the light switch, hoping the
bulb still has life, hoping
the floor isn't damp and
the electrical panel has
survived the storm.

Poets & Painters/ Reflections: July 29

People
love painters;
They love Renoir and
Monet. They love Jackson Pollak
and Henri Matisse.
Painters get a pass
that poets don't.
You can hang a painting
on a wall - but
poems are assembled into books
and hurried off to dusty shelves.

Poets
are scoundrels;
absurd aristocrats;
poor listeners and alcoholics,
night workers and day laborers.
They are farm help and drug store clerks.
They're truck drivers and shit faced bar patrons.
Poetry is after hours. Painting is afternoon at the lake.

Painters
live for light. Good poets work in the dark. Poets die in
New York City and Los Angeles. Painters
die anywhere they choose.

A good poet has no idea
from which direction death
will come. It might be a cold night in Baltimore
or a wet afternoon in Chelsea.

Good painters have
known the score for
decades.

Van Gogh saw it coming.
Damned revolvers.

RIP Vincent Van Gogh: July 29, 1890

Last night in Key West

Unplug the blender.

Pack the Keys disease, &
haul in the bikini, Patricia.
The games are over. No
more days playing nights
no more sand seeking shovels.

Philly awaits, so can
Margaritaville & print the
boarding passes & order
a cappuccino,

the Old Order Amish
knew what they were doing.
Stay close to home
and ride in a buggy.

Fun is relative. 3 hours
in the air is all it takes.
You could write a song
you could discover a myth,
remake cocktail napkins.
Fortune will forsake you,
and sobriety will crush you.

The old man finds you whether you're
looking for him or not.
You'll give up the Ghost
before Big Torch Key goes down.
You'll be buying the condo

in Vail before Islamorada is
under water.
You've a decade to party.

Horizon line

We're in rented
beach chairs on
Pompano Beach,
it's late November – two days
before Thanksgiving
when she asks me how far it is
to the horizon
and I tell her it is 3 miles
give or take a foot or two…

I further explain:

…that it's 3 miles from the point
where her lavender painted
toes touch the water
to where the water touches the sky.

I go on:

That's fifteen thousand
eight hundred forty
feet I say to her —
from your toe tips to
horizon line

then I say…

That's one foot
for every year that
we've known each other…

she laughs

then she tells me that I am not
the world's most renown

mathematician.

You're no Euclid, she says
you're no Blaise Pascal,
no Pythagoras, and
certainly you are no
Archimedes…

then she tells me that
we've known each other
much, much longer than that

Named storms and hurricanes

I'm on my porch
waiting for the end.
I am drinking a bourbon, because it is made
from corn, from the Midwest where I was born.

where the hurricanes were far away and we
listened to the radio for storm reports of
downed barns and bridges washed out
no hurricanes in North Platte or Scotts Bluff
just empty plains stretching away for
a couple of hundred miles toward Wyoming
and Billings, Montana.

No thought of a
storm with a name – what would you
name it? Cody, or Laramie?

Would you
board up the chicken shed,

Put away the
tools?

So we wait for 45 more storms here
in my home in the tropics.

It is
hot here

there are disturbances off
of Africa – across the Atlantic Ocean.
We can bury the dead where they fall,
we can prepare and fear, we can

wait for September where there is
a lot of lead time. Such a big ocean

On the road to Brush Trail

My password expired today,
or so they said,
I was busy reading an article
about Brussel sprouts and
another about the
death of Dylan Thomas.
And another about the Hollywood sign.
There is a hiking trail, just so
you know — Brush Canyon Trail.
It takes you to the sign.
We will hike it someday, you
& me. In better times.
Today I want to
trade a stock that I read about
drinking late one night and the
guy who said the pick was solid
was the same guy who said that :
"All the Gold in California" by
the Gatlin Brothers was the best
fucking song ever written.
I listen to it on my vintage
Walkman, hiking, mornings near
Mt. Pocono.
Now, we are almost on the trail again.
No cell phones, Sweetie.
No technology.
We are in the Scouts,
pioneering our way through the
Rocky Mountain West.

Put one foot ahead of the other.
We are like Lewis and Clark
trying to find the Pacific.

You and me.
We are trying to find the
best place to buy Brussel
sprouts in Long Beach, look it up you say
to me
"it is at your fingertips Mr. Clark"

Lesser mountains

Clamber up the ladder
&
rest your elbows on the ledge
don't overthink your next breath
consider the Himalayas —
they're mountains you'll never visit.

Forget K2; think Polecat Peak.
Forget Everest; think Stowe,
think Mount Sunflower
and Oklahoma High Top.

The Great Peaks are beyond you.

Forever silence is a decade away.
It stings and you
hear it when you bed
down at night, near
the horses…

So, circle the wagons.

Wear your best hat to Safeway
&
flirt with the checkout girl
she won't remember you.

Vegetables are your solace.
Cheap wine is your friend.

Seneca is your confident,
Beethoven is for late night
Strauss is for morning.

Scratch that lottery ticket
& try to buy your way out,
or, have your body
quick frozen in one of those stainless steel
tanks
out in Michigan (think Mount Curwood)
and wait for the cure
to arrive in the 34th century.

you could wake
to a dozen or more years of this.

Screen door: 1971

Screen door – I miss you.
I miss your frame,

your spring,
your hook
your eye.
Man, that's a door
for the ages.
Hang it outside in the
storm and wait.

You won't keep out the drunks,
or the memories.
Or the dirt from the past,
or the gravel dust from the road,
or the bad blood or
daylight.
You won't keep out,
Aunt Laura.
But you do a
good job with the
insects.

You allow the first breath of
spring to waft in across the
mud porch.
How they slam you,
you damned old
green, painted – bastard.
But after midnight
I close you gently, old relic
from 1955.
You creak
like petrified bones headed for the
graveyard.

In the daytime, I'd let you fly
fast and hard – wood on wood.

The day I left home
I closed you for the last time.
I was smoking then
I had a suitcase
from Montgomery Wards,
and a half dozen 8 track
tapes.

You Locked behind me
as
I drove the Ford Fairlane
north
out of town

My July

You remember July like
you've lived it
for ten thousand years.
Since before the buffalo
roamed the Great Plains.
Since before the ice bridge.
Remember July 1973 when
you discovered Truman Capote:
In Cold Blood.

You: reading
and tearing off the pages
while parked in your 1967 Ford
three quarter ton truck.
Ten miles outside of Topeka.
Broke. Nowhere to go.
Capote: The Best damned writer of the 20th century.
How many miles to Holcomb, Kansas?
Heat wave full on – screw the heat,
and barking dogs.

Remember grain sorghum and
Oat straw.
Twisters.
And fear of lightning,
And 45 caliber guns.
In July, it's all better
after dark.
Fireworks and snakes,
and all the things that
pile up on the front lawn.

Sparklers and trash.
Locals moving on to jobs out west.
Sleazy salesmen selling properties
on the lake.
Pontoon boats & fishing gear.
First things first.

You should
have hitchhiked across the USA
and written a book.
There are few days left --
so enjoy the ride to the
beach, enjoy your
life to the end but do not
confront my July

The logger

When I was ten, I wanted
to be a lumberjack.
There was a picture
I saw in a book — 2 guys
on a two man cross cut-saw,
cutting down a tree bigger
than the business district
of Champaign, Illinois.
God give me a saw, and give me
the woods, I said.

The woods
live forever. There is no end to
the trees.
They've been growing for
6 billion years.
Saw them down.
All of them.
Take me with you
if you can.
Take me out west.
To big tree country.
Fuck the plains
and North Dakota, there's
too much dirt.
And screw Long Beach,
there's too much water.
I've no fear of flying, or trains.
Drop me off in Kalispell.
Lend me a hundred
dollars, old pal, so I can
live off the land.

ii

Oregon —
is the promised land —
I'll take a bus
to Bend.
I'll wait tables
and take hotel
reservations.
I will wait for the last of them
to leave town.
I'll keep a bag packed, for I
pack like a prophet.
I read the Bible
and the Book of Mormon.
I'm a Buddhist by faith.

iii

In time,
I will take my axe deep into the
woods and chop until
I am blind. Until I find nirvana
or Jesus or the Saints.

Or until I cross the river
into Portland.
I'll see my day's work loaded onto
flatbed trailers. Pulled by
Peterbilt and Kenworth
tractors and
Trucked down icy
mountain roads.

A lumberjack am I.

I want to watch the timber
disappear south toward
Klamath Falls.

iv.
My aunt Lana's husband,
Gideon, was a lumberjack.
and part time preacher.

He drove
cable cars in San Francisco
in the 1950s, then one day
he quit his job and
drove up to Washington State
in an Edsall car and got a job
as a logger. He must have
cut a million trees
and became a world
class logger.
He bought a house in Enumclaw
and he died there in 1971
a happy man

v

Ten years later, in
the bowls of Manhattan,
they told me I was
Killing trees.
"Back away from that copier
young man" said a mid-level manager.
Your 440-page document
does not need to be copied in triplicate
— think of the planet. Tree killer, you
need to find a job that fits you.

Beach run

You're running on the beach
at sunrise.
Be careful cowboy.
You've got 65 years on those lungs,
but you're doing damn good
for an ex-smoker.
(with 27 million packages of
king sized mentholated
lights behind you),
'Gasp' is not a word
you want some vandal to
spray paint on
your
tombstone.
'Fear' is just another storm,
cloud hanging,
3 and a half,
miles out on
the horizon line.

You were born to sail,

but they handed you

Nebraska.

Sail on.

You needed sky but they

handed you Boodles gin and

midtown.

Pillage on.

You old buccaneer...

you've no disease. You're

good for ten more years

maybe 11.

No shoes necessary

today

clop thru the sand

like one of those old

Central Park carriage

horses.

The haze will burn

off by

9am.

Push on.

Until you feel like that

Bourbon Street

trombone player

you

met

in

1983

the

morning

after

Mardi

Gras

then she's there,

standing over you,

the lady in the hat

with the small dog,

and she asks if you need help.

Lie to her,

and say you've been doing this

for twenty years

maybe 21

Rethinking art school

They want the best for us
don't they?
Remember
the teacher
who told you
that your work
reminded her
of Paul Cezanne
and you thought of
that lady
in her
green hat.

And you think that you
would have painted her
differently…
…you would have
softened the tones
drawn her out, &

…pulled that amused
expression
into a bemused smile…
…but you
knew in a flash

(13 years later)
that you didn't paint
like anyone in
particular…

you knew it then
didn't you…
that you

couldn't paint anything
wouldn't paint anything
refused to paint anything

of great worth

AND

You'd fail at art
and data entry
lock smith-ing
and telemarketing
and finally
computer programming.
And you'd come to deal
with all of that,
in good time,
and you'd find yourself
conveniently
the misplaced
driver of the year
for the most prestigious
trucking company in
Denver.

Has the booze caught up with you yet?

...no way, Cowboy,
You're driving a 1954 Studebaker
aren't you?

Old John Barleycorn
doesn't have a chance.
You've taken on West Hollywood
haven't you? and Kansas City?
You've lived through
the Eisenhower years,
And the Kennedy years,
Nixon and impeachment,
Farm crisis, energy crisis,
big oil, big crash, pharma-bros,
and three downsizings.
You need two hands to
count the wars...

You've survived,
(for the most part)
with a good bourbon
in one hand and a
Grain Belt beer in the other.
So, pay off your tab.
But forget closing time,
like age, it's just a number.
Winners stay in for the
long haul – you have to.
Life is a one-way street.
No way to turn back
after they turn off the
lights. Freeway's closed.

Has the booze caught up
with you yet?
Don't be discouraged,
there is enough high-life
to go around.

So don't despair – you have
new tires on the '54 Stude –
Stomp on it if you want.
She'll do a hundred five,
on a cool night.

Wartorn

Run and hide,
or stay and fight,
there is a Great War on,
and we've all enlisted.

From 37,000 feet Illinois
is laid out like a stamp collection,
below, a million farmers
plant soybeans,
a billion hogs suffer in the heat,
sixteen billion chickens lay eggs
– truck drivers haul loads &
commerce moves like gears
in a great machine – the price of pork bellies soar
oats are forever a safe bet –
I think about derivatives,
futures and swaps
an old farmer chugs down
a limestone road on a John Deere tractor as
I watch Good Morning America
from a motel near St. Louis
as a retired iron worker
wakes to strong black coffee and to
smoke leisurely on the porch
of a clapboard house near the river
reading the news,
fighting emphysema,
thinking about the sixties
the big war,
the last war,
first love,
last love,
a lost lung,

and divorce.

He told his son once,
about the St. Louis Arch
– the highest man-made
arch in the World
– highest damned building
in the state of Missouri
but the son didn't care much
for high-steel
– he was fighting with an ex-wife
& with the IRS;
working for a real SOB
at the brickyard and driving a
12 year old car –
Son wrote the old-man off as a loser years before
– half-baked and battle scared.

After it's too late

Most things we find out about,
after it's too late:
the cop in the bushes
at the bottom
of the hill leading out of town,
the trick question on the exam,
the angry ex-husband,
the tired trucker,
the overworked accountant,
the agitated barber,
the lady with the strange perfume,
in the crowded elevator,
the strange weeds growing in,
the nasturtiums,
the odor in the 'fridge',
the photo she left behind,
the snake in the woodpile,
the match in the trash,
the lock that sticks,
the blind man in the crosswalk,
the codicil in the will,
the tickle in your throat,
the persistent cough,
the round in the chamber.
We think we know it all because,
we get off easy so many times,
that we think we can do it
forever

An inch closer to the flame

Was that death I heard downstairs,
rattling the pots & pans.
Was that My Maker I spotted,
on South Ocean Avenue with his thumb out,
hitching north toward Mar-a-Lago.
Was that a congressman I spied,
in the light of the quarter moon,
reading from the collected works,
of a great poet long gone on,
to his literary reward?
Let's drink gin and discuss the market,
and the rise of the hedge fund cowboys,
and their three thousand-dollar shoes.

Press on.

Make sure the great and
glorious fires of freedom remain stoked.
Make your peace with the Big Guy,
but there is no need to go overboard.
You've had decades to explore Buddhism,
plenty of time to clean out the cobwebs,
maybe give up the booze.
Don't let them talk you into anything,
you don't need another vacuum cleaner,
another Volkswagen, or another juicer…

For crying out loud,
there hasn't been a decent
communist, walking
42nd Street since 1956…
The Beats are dead.
The hippies have retired to Martha's Vineyard
and to the Hamptons – and Sag Harbor.

Nobody reads the poets anymore.
Poetry doesn't sell.
Reality sells…reality TV sells better.
Old men in suits sell reality TV.
Old poets die in overstuffed chairs
by the fire – the lucky ones.

Cleveland

Cleveland is down there,
thirty-six thousand feet below,
says the pilot.
But I don't see Cleveland.
I see blue-grey Ohio haze.
Pink afternoon clouds
in the late afternoon
sunlight.
It's 3 days before Christmas.
I'm flying east, the mid-west
quickly giving way to the
east coast.
I look again for Cleveland…
I see the Lake –
but no Cleveland.
I think that God is a lot like Cleveland.
Tough to spot sometimes,
but probably there.
For five or ten minutes,
religion makes sense.

On writing a poem

Writing a poem is often like,
pushing a wheelbarrow full of bricks,
up a steep hill,
for absolutely no reason, whatsoever.

Nobody really needs the bricks,
nobody cares if you make it to the top,
or if you spill half of the load,
on the way up.

In the end, you'll be just,
another forlorn, and tired,
wheelbarrow pusher,
you'll never be a bricklayer.

If you were a bricklayer,
you'd write a novel,
and carry your bricks up one at a time,
and arrange them very carefully.

But you're no bricklayer – so,
be content with your task,
concentrate on the load,
rejoice at the summit.

Gathering shells

How many shells wash in from the sea
a million and one? A million and three?
how many grains of sand to fill your pail
how much wind to hoist a sail
how much fire to burn a forest
how much cash to lift the poorest
how much time till it's all over
how many bees in a field of clover
how many answers fall on deaf ears
how many prayers end in our tears

The fence

Last night I dreamed,
that I was building a fence,
– a sturdy wooden fence.
I was dressed in leather gloves,
and an engineer's cap,
and brown, duck-bib overalls.

I stood alone in the early spring sun,
hammering ten-penny nails,
into hand-hewn plank,
after hand-hewn plank, -- pound, pound,
– board against hedge post,
level it up, then pound some more,
–sweat dripping from the tip of my beard.

"What a great fence," I hear someone
shout from the edge of the pasture.
But I pay no attention to him.
"Join us for drinks at 5 another yells out."
"Your ass is on the line," says still another…
I ignore them all.
I am immersed in
a project that can be finished with brute force,
with only fresh spring water,
needed for replenishment,
out here on the Frontier,
far from the cocktail bar,
and corporate conference room.

So confident in my keen sense of detail,
and hand-to-eye coordination am I,
that I barely notice,
the Finish Line in view,

driving one nail after the next…
my back aching from unloading planks,
and aligning them properly,
scarcely stopping to smell,
the nightingale, and the forsythia,
pound, pound – the Great Western Wall,
between marauding Angus steers,
and the berry patch,
is nearly complete.

But I awake to incompetence.
No forsythia, planks, berries, or steers.
Only a flashing cursor on an empty, white screen,
and the sound of traffic rushing past,
on the street ten floors below.

Don't change a thing

Don't change a thing,
please don't move
the McCoy pottery vase,
that has stood,
on the cherry wood table,
in the front room for the past 16 years,
leave it where it is.

…Leave the paper roses,
where you found them,
on the porch swing,
crumpled and soaked,
in port wine.
Leave the keys to the,
'75 Chrysler New Yorker on the
Grand Hotel Key Rack
beside the basement
stairs. Remember,
it's all in the details,
so don't move anything,
if you don't have to.
…
Pretend,
it's morning again.
So just – roll over,
it's only 8 am,
sleep for another hour,
after all, the trains,
don't run on Sunday.
Later on,
we'll take the dogs out,
and let them run,
along the shore of the lake.

Just don't change a thing,
I'll turn my hat around,
and wear it backwards,
and I will offer you a clove cigarette,
and a cup of black coffee.

We'll walk to,
the railroad bridge,
and we will turn our backs,
to the summer wind,
but we won't change,
a damned thing,
ever, if we know,
what's good for us.

The dilemma

Life is habit,
most of it…
some bad,
some good.
Remember that girl, Louisa,
that you hung with
when you were,
right out of high school,
and filled,
with habit-forming bravado.
When you were
dreaming about,
flying airplanes,
and surfing in
Honduras.
And you spent
hours discussing
your future plans
with her over Grain Belt Premium
… She was habit.
When she left town
saying that she
had no time for Honduras
and was scared
as shit of flying,
you continued
with the next
habit.

ii

The Chesterfields
and chilled white wine…

those two saw you through,
mid-town and on,
into the outer boroughs,
until you found yourself…
…clinging to a capsized
dingy one night,
floating in the center of the Hudson River.

Life is habit,
most of it,
some bad,
some good.
You spend a lot of life,
at Trader Joe's,
in the produce aisle,
inspecting romaine lettuce,
and selecting limes.
You spend a lot of life,
at the convenience store,
weekday mornings,
at 5:45AM
pouring scalding black coffee into,
a flimsy paper cup.
Habits all.
And now you're pissed off,
that your middle finger is,
burned and can't be used
for at least a week,
and you think that you will be
doing this,
every day… from now,
until the next century
and you can't imagine it any other way …

iii

You're an old wrangler herding cows,
you're an old surfer looking for a 50 foot wave,
you're an old farmer waiting for rain,
you're an old poet, listening to the dogs snore,
under the table, as Chopin plays on the stereo,
as you stare at a page on your yellowing legal pad,
waiting for a scene to drop by, so you can give it life.

It's habit.
You think that you will be doing this,
until the day that you die,
and you probably will,
because there's no way out

The Florida Derby

i

Once, I wanted to paint
but the canvas
wasn't there
I found, instead
just an old bed sheet
that someone
had left out in the
early morning
Miami rain…
…poor visibility
port wine
and cataracts
cloud my
judgement.

ii

I find comfort in
your arms when
the weather beats
against the shutters,
when the old
drunks clatter
down the street
at 4AM
when there is
a truck abandoned
at the end of the block
with its lights still on
when

a life is lost
or
a soul forgotten.

iii

I think of a shipwreck
twenty years ago
…I dream of youth
and riding the finest
horse in the world
across the finish line.
We've never lost a race yet,
have we?

Outside the box

About that box...
There is a middle level manager.
Who told you to think outside of it.

But he didn't mean it. Not really.
Maybe he meant it at the time
– at 3PM last Thursday.

Outside the box is a world
that exists only to satisfy the reckless and
those holding on to the hope of a check
in the bank next week.

There is plenty of life
outside the box, but...
...they switched boxes on you.

The real box
is long gone
...having been
lashed to the deck
of Senegalese freighter,
which has long since lost power,
and drifted
off the coast of Portugal for a
week and a half before taking on water
and going down in twenty-foot seas.

No survivors.

That box is now at the bottom of the sea.

Lift me up

Sometimes it is more about blind luck
than it is about perseverance.
Sometimes it is more about grace,
than beauty,
more about class than
canned, recycled elegance.
You know what I mean
you've watched the
stars and the starlets,
and read the right Magazines.
You've read Nietzsche, and
Hemingway – after that, what's left?
You've been scared as hell
in the night, and
yet you've welcomed
the dark.
Tonight, I am going to
read "Death in the Afternoon".

I need a lift.

Anger

Don't stay angry for too long,
you can be mad for a while,
that's the way of the world,
we were made to be that way,
we were made to stay,
pissed off for 2 or 3 days,
not much more…

… in the end, there's no room
for any of it.

Forget that swindler who
resurfaced your driveway.
Forget the woman in the red Audi
who cut you off on the freeway.
Forget the guy from Corporate
who outsourced your job to Bangalore.
Forget about cell phone overage charges,
And the price of bottled water,

…unless they mess with your dog

let it go.

The corporate ladder

"don't worry about your place
on the corporate ladder,
there will always be some fucker
down there, two rungs below
...rubbing two sticks together
– trying to start the fire
to burn you down"

or so says Gus, the new bartender
at the Los Lobos Bar,
but what does he know (I tell myself)
damned bartenders
and their sage words,

all of 'em

trying to sound like they
know things the rest of us don't
trying to act like they
have done it all about two
weeks before the rest of us

...they think they're a sounding board
for the desperate
and they think that we have no place
left to go

Gus asks if I want one more
before he gets busy
with the lunch crowd
but I wave him off
saying I have to get
back to
the office

Tax time

Naked
and afraid?
Who, you?
me?
Not a chance
dig your
pink painted toes
into the sand and
file the extension.

Then kiss me
like we have no
real chance
of going home.

It's a two and
a half hour
flight to
Tegucigalpa, so
call up the relatives
and pretend
there's a new investor
named Ferdinand
and he's burning
cash like there
is no tomorrow.

Just kiss me
again and
say if there
is such a thing
as real love

you've found it here
on deadbeat beach.

In a week we will
be on the bus
to Choluteca
drinking warm beer
and laughing about
the last check we
left for the
landlord.

Upper Keys bagel poem

…can't be that bad…
the skiff is still afloat
the shadows have
hastened away, and
you and I are upright
as well…
and waiting for the next
thing to happen
AS we wait for the
quiet of mid-morning
to slink in like some
old washed up
guitar player,
like some has-been
drugged out rock star
like some careless,
flat-busted, fishing guide.

We wait until the traffic slows
on the OS Highway
so we can walk up to the
bagel shop where that
guy named Nigel says
he has the best damned
bagels south of Brooklyn
but you say he hasn't got
a clue as to what goes
into a bagel
you tell me that he's
too self-absorbed.
You tell me
there is not
a fucking

bagel
worth
eating
south of Cape May, New Jersey.

We eat our bagels
in peace – on the deck
of the best damned
Brooklyn Bagel dive
in the Upper Keys.

You wave to
some driver in
a furniture truck
barreling
south on US 1
you tell me, that
he's driving too fast
and in the end
it's all just another
accident waiting
to happen.

Old soul

I once read about a doctor,
who said the human soul,
weighs 21 grams ...
and smells like old vegetables.
"Bat-shit quack" I thought at
the time.
Who weighs a soul?

But today, I think the Doc is right.
I can feel my soul
rustling around --
...anxious to get on with it.
He's restless,
my soul.
He needs Cajun food.
He needs a book by
Norman Mailer.
He needs Picasso.
He needs a damn good
poem.

Soul would like to hike,
the Appalachian Trail,
but he'll settle for an
Algonquin Bloody Mary.
No politics today -
the soul won't stand for it.
Soul needs 1960's reruns on TV:
    F-Troop -
    Hazel, maybe Topper.

Or put Kitty Wells on
the boom box:
   "It Wasn't God Who Made Honky Tonk Angels"
He wants out -- my soul.
On frigid winter mornings,
he sleeps in, but not today.
Today he taps his fist against the
backside of my ribcage.
He's a pushy old soul.

Emboldened spirits peer
over the limestone walls of the
graveyard across the street,
and wonder what's keeping us.

Fix Spring

Of all of it, God, fix Spring first,
It is not long enough and
the miserable April rains are a lot to
slosh through on my way
to the Farmers' market.

Are you talking to God again
you old agnostic, she says to me.

You barely observe Christmas,
And now you want a fix for Spring,
You've some nerve…

You should be asking for peace
In the middle east,
not a clear path to the organic radishes.

You should be asking about the state
of your soul,
You believe in a soul don't you?
You old Radish

God, you've moved your moon

God, you've moved your moon,
and I was the last one to see it go,
but I had nothing to do with it,
you probably decided it was in
the wrong spot all along
you probably wanted to…

…push those tides in another direction,
after all, who cares about the coastline?
Fragile, my eye, it'll wash away
in another hundred thousand years.
Screw the migratory birds too
they were more trouble than they were worth.
Give them space, they'll find somewhere to nest
where it's warm – the New Yorkers do —

it's called Miami Beach.

To hell with the dolphins, what good are they
to the people in Cincinnati and Tulsa
and Paducah, it makes no difference in the Great End!

After all, we are all just casual victims of circumstance
aren't we? We didn't ask for any of it…
yet, here we are, misunderstood and praying for daylight
huddled under blankets and
hiding in the backseat of an '85 Buick
as the great 21st Century manhunt thunders
through the Streets like those Pamplona bulls

…stay ahead of them if you can fella'
it's a young man's game — not for the
old and rickety…not for the faint of heart

you are but a step away
from death by horn or hoof.

So phone the Vicar, let's get to the bottom of it,
write a poem, write a song,
Garcia is long gone, we're on our own.

Wine glass in winter

there's a wine glass
on the table
on the back porch

by the swing
beside the flour bin
beside the feed sacks
that the cats sleep on

Sadie left it

one afternoon
last fall
when she stopped by
to drink
port wine
with me
and to tell me that she was
quitting drinking
in 72 hours
and to let me know that
she'd decided to forget
"the regimen"
and she was going to tell
the doctors in Philly
that she was going to
move on with her
new life
…in Scottsdale

and
when she left
that day
..she didn't
rub the tummy
of the Buddha

that sits on the shelf
by
the back steps
and she didn't
pick up
Lancelot and kiss him
behind the ears
or toss her hair
over her left
shoulder
or remind me to pay
my phone bill…
…I knew she was
gone, so I
left the wine glass

…on the table

where it collects
winter light
at half past three
in the afternoon.

next month
I'll bring it in
and wash it
and put it away
but for now it is too
cold for me
to leave
the kitchen
and the
cats

So, today
I'll think of
Sadie in her

sundress
drinking
saying that
if she had another year
she'd
go out to Michigan
and look up her old man
and her daughter
but at the present time
she didn't think she had it
in her

Midnight at the planetarium

Is that Jupiter out there smiling down on us?
Knowing we'll be here for a few scant years
at best. A saintly old man in a cardigan
passes by, smelling of whiskey and pipe
tobacco and you whisper he looks like
Einstein---with that head of hair - and then Venus
comes into play, and tiny whispers
circulate thru the Milky Way,
so, you touch my arm, and I can smell
sweet Sagittarius in your hair, and a touch
of the Aurora Borealis is reflecting from your
rosy cheeks. We are all travelers says Einstein,
and he takes off his spectacles and tells us
Tolstoy was a Virgo, and we consult the sky map.
You are radiant, and I am consumed in stodgy details:
Show me the rings of Saturn if you dare, I say.
But you name the moons of Jupiter instead: Io, Europa, Ganymede,
Callisto.

I'm still computing distance; your breath
is like the first sip of summer wine
and we sit on a precipice high
over the New Mexico mountains and we say to each other
that one day I will be going north,
and you will be going south.
We ignore the clock and turn our
attention to the rim of the galaxy and deep
deep space and the chasm between us.

Afraid of Ghosts

I'm afraid of ghosts.
...I see them,

before I go to sleep
they wear old hats
and they walk along the
fence rows of
Nebraska cornfields
in late afternoon
and they sit in the
cabs of ancient trucks
parked along the
back fence of an
Oklahoma cement plant
...I see one now...
chewing on a straw
and another smoking
a Camel cigarette.

I see them
playing cards
with a horse-faced
guy named Mercer
in a Winnebago Brave
that sits alongside
a wrecking yard
in South Chicago, and
I see them
picking their way
carefully - across the
tracks in a
train yard in Kansas City
and...I see them

in

a board room of a Wall Street
bank – leering ---
at the opposition
as if to see all the way
through her cream colored
skirt and all the way to
Shanghai
where it is a new
Banking day

I hear them predict their own
demise
at a cocktail party in South Hampton
then I hear them predict
their next wife
and then
their next drink
and I hear them laugh
at the prospect of
their eventual
incarceration
Old ghosts rise from

the tin blue water of
a lake
in northwest,
Minnesota
where
my cousin Mitchell died
in 1963,
I see them
sulking in the hallways of
a morgue
in Oregon
where they brought David
after he put a bullet
through his left eye 22 years
ago, and

I see them
deplaning -- single file from
a flight from Southeast Asia,
back in 1969
I see them

in my dreams
when it's too late
to sleep
and too early to
drink...
...the old soldiers
the old dogs
the pieces-of-eight
the forty pieces
of silver
the
trunk of gold bullion,
that sits at the bottom
of the ocean
a hundred sixty miles
off the coast of Honduras

I see
the farmers, the
miners
the
drinkers and fighters

I see
lovers and thinkers
the writers and
the scorned painters
the castaways and
the forlorn
...and the
suicidal hookers
and the near death

actors
and,
...
The solemn
preachers
and the snake-oil salesmen

...I see cowboys, drinking
Falstaff beer
and cussing at horses
long after the rodeo
has left town.

I'm afraid of
them all.

Stick shift

I miss most
that sweet interaction
of the gears. The meshing
delicate transaction
between left foot and
right hand.

That measured
practiced man machine
handshake.
Click-clack
in we go.

Open the vents
there's sweet summer
air to breathe.
The butts of
two dozen Pall Malls are
crushed in the ashtray...
a halfmoon is rising over
the Kansas turnpike
Gas and go. August is on
the move. There is no time
to waste -- Kerouac rode
this wave once didn't he?
All the way to the Pacific
and back again...

"Lookout" someone shouts
from the radio – "time is not
on your side old boy".

Soon you'll go the way of
the Conestoga
wagon and
the DC3 Airplane.
You'll be a museum piece,
hobbled and shelved.
Relegated to the chance discovery
by the curious under grad or
basement bound computer nerd.

Let the countdown begin,
drop it into high...you're
moving as fast as you can now.
Don't overdrive your lights.
Remember her now, with wheat fields
on two sides and a concrete
runway stretching ahead all
the way to the Santa Monica
pier...

ABOUT THE AUTHOR

w e patterson is a native mid-westerner who currently resides in Melbourne Beach, Florida with his wife Mary Jane and his golden retriever Schooner. A technical writer by profession, he is the author of the novella "The DUI Guy". His first poetry collection "outrunning the storm" appeared in 2014. He blogs at:

edsendoftheplanetbooks.com

www.ingramcontent.com/pod-product-compliance
Lightning Source LLC
LaVergne TN
LVHW050608100826
845148LV00015B/3185

* 9 7 9 8 2 1 8 0 4 2 7 6 9 *